LAWRENCE WELK'S  POLKA

for PIANO and
PIANO ACCORDION

Contents

Title	Page
Ariana Polka	15
Around The Loop Polka	22
Artist's Life	32
Barbara Polka	4
Birthday Greeting Polka	61
Blue Danube Waltz	30
Blue Eyes	29
Bridegroom Polka	33
Budweiser Polka	9
Canteen Polka	39
Carnival Of Venice	42
Clarinet Polka	2
Crackerjack Polka	63
Cuckoo Polka	3
Dolores	47
The Dove Polka	17
Draw One Polka	56
Engagement Polka	51
Espana	47
Estudiantina	46
Favorite Strauss Waltzes	30
Free Lunch	43
Gold And Silver	40
Gypsy Polka	62
Hay Seed Schottische	18
Heel And Toe Polka	64
Helena Polka	26
The Hornpipe Polka	7

Title	Page
I Met A Nice Girl	11
International Waltzes	40
Katinka Polka	48
Let's Have Another One	13
Little Brown Jug	19
Martha Polka	60
Nickelodian Polka	28
Old Fashioned Polka	34
Oldtimer's Waltz Medley	36
O Susanna	20
Over The Waves	41
Picnic Polka	54
Private Jones Polka	44
Red Handkerchief	52
Saxophone Polka	57
Schnitzelbank	6
Shuffle Schottische	24
The Skaters	46
Sleigh Bell Polka	55
Squeeze Box Polka	59
Take It Easy Polka	50
Tales From The Vienna Woods	31
There's A Tavern In The Town	35
Vienna Life	30
Vilia	41
Waldteufel Waltzes	46
Where Is My Baby?	10
Windy City Polka	14

ISBN 978-0-7935-3399-2

HAL•LEONARD®
CORPORATION

7777 W. BLUEMOUND RD. P.O. BOX 13819 MILWAUKEE, WI 53213

Visit Hal Leonard Online at
www.halleonard.com

NOTE FOR ACCORDIONISTS:
For the left hand, follow these signs:
1. Major chord
2. Minor chord
3. Seventh chord
4. Diminished chord
-. Counter bass (only for left hand)

Clarinet Polka

LAWRENCE WELK
Arrangement

NOTE FOR ACCORDIONISTS:
For the left hand, follow these signs:
1. Major chord
2. Minor chord
3. Seventh chord
4. Diminished chord
−. Counter bass (only for left hand)

Cuckoo Polka

ETA STOLAR

NOTE FOR ACCORDIONISTS:
For the left hand, follow these signs:
1. Major chord
2. Minor chord
3. Seventh chord
4. Diminished chord
–. Counter bass (only for left hand)

Barbara Polka

F. KOVARIK

Medium Polka

NOTE FOR ACCORDIONISTS:
For the left hand, follow these signs:
1. Major chord
2. Minor chord
3. Seventh chord
4. Diminished chord
−. Counter bass (only for left hand)

Schnitzelbank

LAWRENCE WELK
Arrangement

Medium Polka

NOTE FOR ACCORDIONISTS:
For the left hand, follow these signs:
1. Major chord
2. Minor chord
3. Seventh chord
4. Diminished chord
–. Counter bass (only for left hand)

The Hornpipe Polka

FRANK SMITH

Medium Polka

8

NOTE FOR ACCORDIONISTS:
For the left hand, follow these signs:
1. Major chord
2. Minor chord
3. Seventh chord
4. Diminished chord
–. Counter bass (only for left hand)

Budweiser Polka

G. STEVENS

NOTE FOR ACCORDIONISTS:
For the left hand, follow these signs:
1. Major chord
2. Minor chord
3. Seventh chord
4. Diminished chord
-. Counter bass (only for left hand)

Where Is My Baby?

HARRY HARDEN

A la Polka

Chorus

I Met A Nice Girl

ETA STOLAR

NOTE FOR ACCORDIONISTS:
For the left hand, follow these signs:
1. Major chord
2. Minor chord
3. Seventh chord
4. Diminished chord
−. Counter bass (only for left hand)

Let's Have Another One

DON RAYE and
HUGHIE PRINCE

NOTE FOR ACCORDIONISTS:
For the left hand, follow these signs:
1. Major chord
2. Minor chord
3. Seventh chord
4. Diminished chord
-. Counter bass (only for left hand)

Windy City Polka

O. SOKOL

NOTE FOR ACCORDIONISTS:
For the left hand, follow these signs:
1. Major chord
2. Minor chord
3. Seventh chord
4. Diminished chord
-. Counter bass (only for left hand)

Ariana Polka

HARRY HARDEN

Medium tempo

Chorus

NOTE FOR ACCORDIONISTS:
For the left hand, follow these signs:
1. Major chord
2. Minor chord
3. Seventh chord
4. Diminished chord
-. Counter bass (only for left hand)

The Dove Polka

B. NOWOTNY

Medium Polka

NOTE FOR ACCORDIONISTS:
For the left hand, follow these signs:
1. Major chord
2. Minor chord
3. Seventh chord
4. Diminished chord
-. Counter bass (only for left hand)

Hay Seed Schottische

DAN. HOWELL

Coda

NOTE FOR ACCORDIONISTS:
For the left hand, follow these signs:
1. **Major chord**
2. **Minor chord**
3. **Seventh chord**
4. **Diminished chord**
-. **Counter bass (only for left hand)**

Little Brown Jug

TRADITIONAL
LAWRENCE WELK Arrangement

Bright Polka

NOTE FOR ACCORDIONISTS:
For the left hand, follow these signs:
1. Major chord
2. Minor chord
3. Seventh chord
4. Diminished chord
-. Counter bass (only for left hand)

O Susanna

W. HINSCH

Bright Polka

NOTE FOR ACCORDIONISTS:
For the left hand, follow these signs:
1. Major chord
2. Minor chord
3. Seventh chord
4. Diminished chord
–. Counter bass (only for left hand)

Around The Loop Polka

E. FRANCES

Medium Polka

NOTE FOR ACCORDIONISTS:

For the left hand, follow these signs:
1. Major chord
2. Minor chord
3. Seventh chord
4. Diminished chord
-. Counter bass (only for left hand)

Shuffle Schottische

STANISLAUS LAUB

Schottische Tempo

Helena Polka

NOTE FOR ACCORDIONISTS:
For the left hand, follow these signs:
1. Major chord
2. Minor chord
3. Seventh chord
4. Diminished chord
-. Counter bass (only for left hand)

Words by
MORT GREENE

Music by
VIC SCHOEN

NOTE FOR ACCORDIONISTS:
For the left hand, follow these signs:
1. Major chord
2. Minor chord
3. Seventh chord
4. Diminished chord
-. Counter bass (only for left hand)

Nickelodian Polka

PETER ANDOWITZ

Bright

Blue Eyes

H. HOBERMAN

NOTE FOR ACCORDIONISTS:
For the left hand, follow these signs:
1. Major chord
2. Minor chord
3. Seventh chord
4. Diminished chord
-. Counter bass (only for left hand)

Favorite Strauss Waltzes

LAWRENCE WELK
Arrangement

"Blue Danube"
A la Viennese

"Vienna Life"

"Tales From The Vienna Woods"

"Artist's Life"

NOTE FOR ACCORDIONISTS:
For the left hand, follow these signs:
1. Major chord
2. Minor chord
3. Seventh chord
4. Diminished chord
–. Counter bass (only for left hand)

Bridegroom Polka

Music by
H. HARDEN

Words by
S. GRAHAM

Bright tempo

Voice

f

p

Where is the bride? Where is the groom?

Let's all see your fac-es through-out the room, Let's cheer the bride,

D7   G7   C7

Let's cheer the groom___ Con grat-u - la-tions ring through the room.___

Eb   Bb   C7   F7   Bb

NOTE FOR ACCORDIONISTS:
For the left hand, follow these signs:
1. Major chord
2. Minor chord
3. Seventh chord
4. Diminished chord
-. Counter bass (only for left hand)

Old Fashioned Polka

FRED SABOTKA

Slow Polka

Trio

Fine

There's A Tavern In The Town

NOTE FOR ACCORDIONISTS:
For the left hand, follow these signs:
1. Major chord
2. Minor chord
3. Seventh chord
4. Diminished chord
–. Counter bass (only for left hand)

LAWRENCE WELK
Arrangement

Fast Polka

Fine 2nd time   G7 3

D.S. al Fine

NOTE FOR ACCORDIONISTS:
For the left hand, follow these signs:
1. Major chord
2. Minor chord
3. Seventh chord
4. Diminished chord
-. Counter bass (only for left hand)

Oldtimer's Waltz Medley

LAWRENCE WELK
Arrangement

"Band Played On"
Moderate Waltz

"Daisy Bell" (On A Bicycle Built For Two)

"Home On The Range"

NOTE FOR ACCORDIONISTS:
For the left hand, follow these signs:
1. **Major chord**
2. **Minor chord**
3. **Seventh chord**
4. **Diminished chord**
-. **Counter bass (only for left hand)**

Canteen Polka

LUDWIG MILLER

Bright

NOTE FOR ACCORDIONISTS.
For the left hand, follow these signs:
1. Major chord
2. Minor chord
3. Seventh chord
4. Diminished chord
-. Counter bass (only for left hand)

International Waltzes

LAWRENCE WELK
Arrangement

Tempo di Viennese
"Gold And Silver" (*Franz Lehar*)

"Vilia" (*Frans Lehar*)

"Over The Waves" (*Juventino Rosas*)

"Carnival Of Venice" (Traditional)

NOTE FOR ACCORDIONISTS:
For the left hand, follow these signs:
1. Major chord
2. Minor chord
3. Seventh chord
4. Diminished chord
−. Counter bass (only for left hand)

Free Lunch

T. FISHER

Schottische Tempo

Private Jones Polka

NOTE FOR ACCORDIONISTS:
For the left hand, follow these signs:
1. Major chord
2. Minor chord
3. Seventh chord
4. Diminished chord
-. Counter bass (only for left hand)

Words by
SID ROBIN

Music by
LOU SINGER

Medium March Polka

NOTE FOR ACCORDIONISTS:
For the left hand, follow these signs:
1. Major chord
2. Minor chord
3. Seventh chord
4. Diminished chord
-. Counter bass (only for left hand)

Waldteufel Waltzes

LAWRENCE WELK
Arrangement

Tempo di Viennese
"The Skaters"

"Estudiantina"

48

Katinka Polka

JOHANN STRAUSS

Medium Polka

NOTE FOR ACCORDIONISTS:
For the left hand, follow these signs:
1. **Major chord**
2. **Minor chord**
3. **Seventh chord**
4. **Diminished chord**
−. **Counter bass (only for left hand)**

Take It Easy Polka

FRITZ FREUD

Medium Polka

Engagement Polka

NOTE FOR ACCORDIONISTS:
For the left hand, follow these signs:
1. Major chord
2. Minor chord
3. Seventh chord
4. Diminished chord
−. Counter bass (only for left hand)

Words by
S. GRAHAM

Music by
H. HARDEN

NOTE FOR ACCORDIONISTS:
For the left hand. follow these signs:
1. Major chord
2. Minor chord
3. Seventh chord
4. Diminished chord
-. Counter bass (only for le.. hand)

Red Handkerchief

B. SANDS

Medium Waltz

NOTE FOR ACCORDIONISTS:
For the left hand, follow these signs:
1. Major chord
2. Minor chord
3. Seventh chord
4. Diminished chord
-. Counter bass (only for left hand)

Picnic Polka

HARRY HARDEN

NOTE FOR ACCORDIONISTS:
For the left hand, follow these signs:
1. Major chord
2. Minor chord
3. Seventh chord
4. Diminished chord
−. Counter bass (only for left hand)

Sleigh Bell Polka

L. LEVANDOWSKI

NOTE FOR ACCORDIONISTS:
For the left hand, follow these signs:
1. Major chord
2. Minor chord
3. Seventh chord
4. Diminished chord
-. Counter bass (only for left hand)

Draw One Polka

K. LUBOW

Medium tempo

Fine 2nd time

Trio

NOTE FOR ACCORDIONISTS:
For the left hand, follow these signs:
1. **Major chord**
2. **Minor chord**
3. **Seventh chord**
4. **Diminished chord**
-. **Counter bass (only for left hand)**

Saxophone Polka

T. FISHER

Medium Polka

NOTE FOR ACCORDIONISTS:

For the left hand, follow these signs:
1. Major chord
2. Minor chord
3. Seventh chord
4. Diminished chord
-. Counter bass (only for left hand)

Squeeze Box Polka

LAWRENCE WELK

Medium Polka

NOTE FOR ACCORDIONISTS:
For the left hand, follow these signs:
1. **Major chord**
2. **Minor chord**
3. **Seventh chord**
4. **Diminished chord**
-. **Counter bass** (only for left hand)

Martha Polka

B. NOWOTNY

Birthday Greeting Polka

NOTE FOR ACCORDIONISTS:
For the left hand, follow these signs:
1. Major chord
2. Minor chord
3. Seventh chord
4. Diminished chord
-. Counter bass (only for left hand)

Words by
S. GRAHAM

Music by
H. HARDEN

Bright tempo — Voice

Birth - day Greet - ing Birth - day Greet - ing there goes an - oth - er year. Birth - day year. Our best of luck to (N - A - M - E____) Our best of luck, From friends who are sin - cere. Let's all drink and have some fun, We stop count - ing at twen - ty - one.

NOTE FOR ACCORDIONISTS:
For the left hand, follow these signs:
1. Major chord
2. Minor chord
3. Seventh chord
4. Diminished chord
-. Counter bass (only for left hand)

Gypsy Polka

C. GAAL

Bright Polka

NOTE FOR ACCORDIONISTS:
For the left hand, follow these signs:
1. Major chord
2. Minor chord
3. Seventh chord
4. Diminished chord
–. Counter bass (only for left hand)

Crackerjack Polka

L. LEDNAM

Medium Polka

NOTE FOR ACCORDIONISTS:
For the left hand, follow these signs:
1. Major chord
2. Minor chord
3. Seventh chord
4. Diminished chord
-. Counter bass (only for left hand)

Heel And Toe Polka

LAWRENCE WELK
Arrangement